All About Pigs

by Margaret Gallo

Harcourt

Orlando   Boston   Dallas   Chicago   San Diego

Visit *The Learning Site!*

www.harcourtschool.com

What have you read about pigs?
You may think pigs are dirty or
not too smart.
Duke, the pig, will tell you a few
facts about pigs.

2

Pigs are cute animals. They are a lot like cats and dogs. A pig has four feet and a short tail.

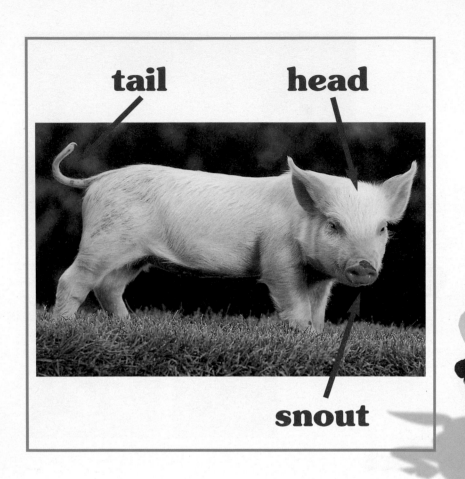
tail head

snout

At the end of a pig's head is a
long snout. Pigs use their snouts
to find food in the ground.

4

A mama pig feeds her baby pigs milk. She cares for her cute young pigs.

Pigs are small when they
are born. Some pigs grow
to be huge.

Some people think pigs are dirty animals. Pigs do spend a lot of time in the mud. Do you know why?

Mud keeps the pigs from getting
too hot.

8

These farm pigs are very
clean. Even cute young pigs
are very clean.

Some people think that pigs
are not too smart, but that is
not right! As a rule, pigs are
very smart.

10

Many pigs can learn tricks.
People even keep pet pigs. They
train a pet pig, just like a dog.

11

This boy brought home a cute little pet pig. He sings a tune to his new pet.

Pigs use grunts to talk to
each other. Each grunt has
a meaning.

There are many kinds of pigs.
Some pigs are one color, other
pigs have spots.

Some pigs are huge. Others are very small. But pigs are the same in many ways.

There is no other animal quite
like a pig. They are very special.